The Bron Yr Aur project
exhibition guide and catalogue

Design and layout: Scott Roe
Front cover: Jim Stallings - 'Direction'

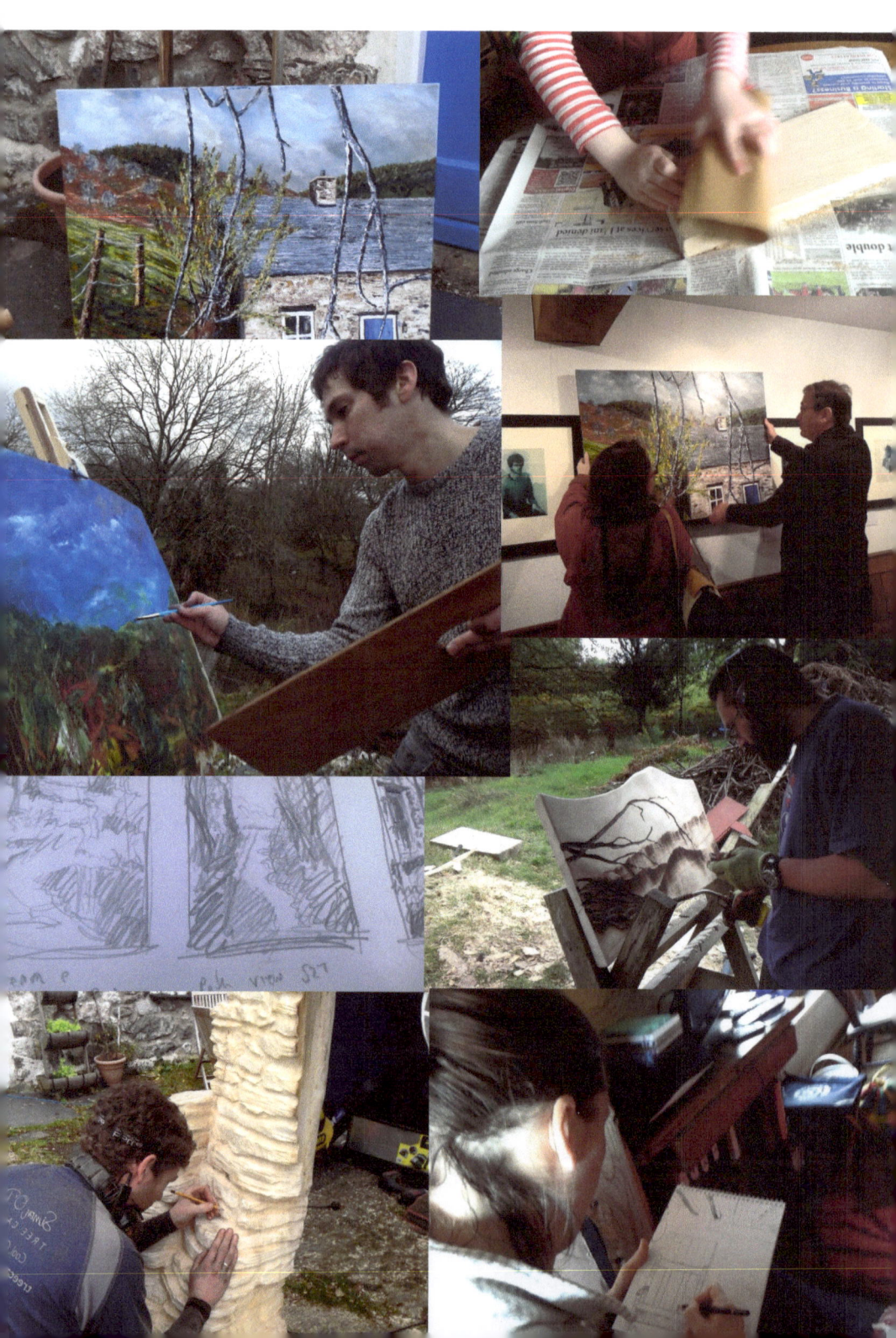

Contents

The Bron Yr Aur Project

Hidden in the hills surrounding Machynlleth, Snowdonia, I have whiled away hours, days and years. In all life's changes I have felt the same slate beneath my feet, heard the same latch on the door, and breathed the same unique combination of bracken, stone and sea-air from the West.

And now these stones and trees that have themselves heard and seen so much, have their essence caught not only in music,but in paint, carving and print, and it is my privilege to be able to share a little piece of my home and heart with you. Jim, Simon, Nathan, Scott, Ben, Tina & White Dove - thankyou. **Ruth @ Bron yr aur.**

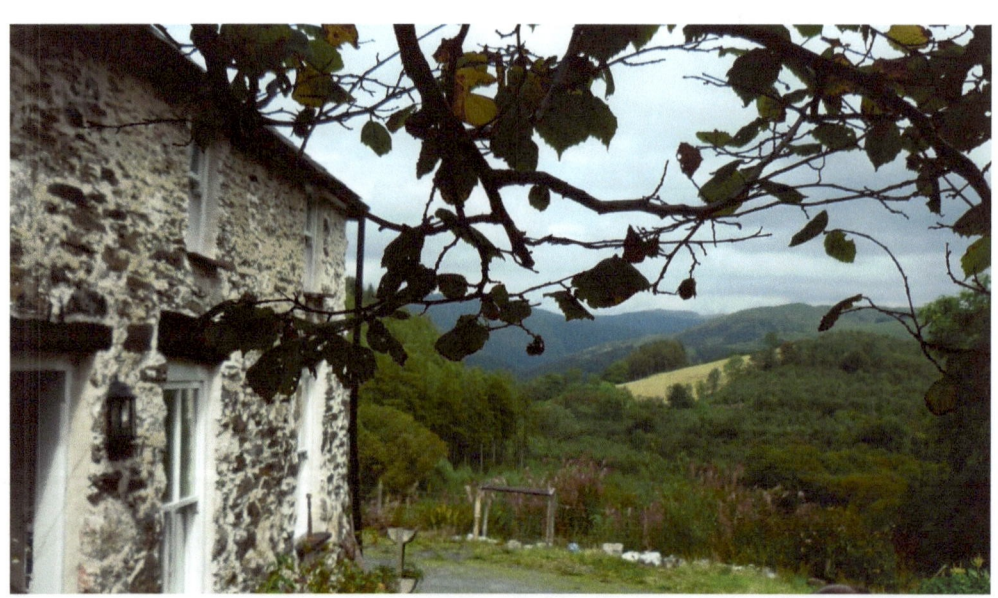

Jim Stallings
Macon, Georgia, USA

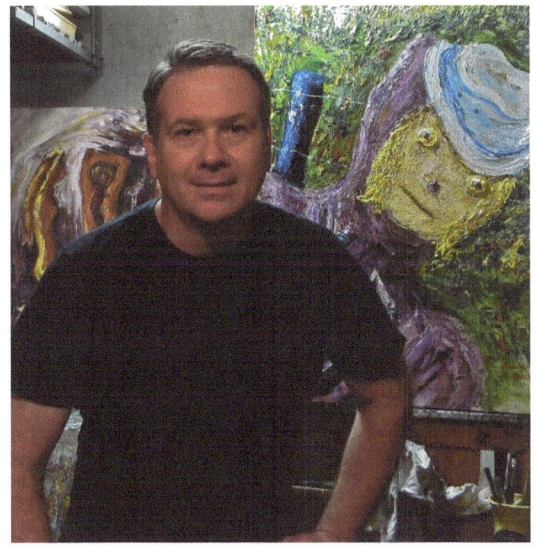

"People often over think art. It's just a lot of energy that comes together in one place".

That has always been a simple way to characterize Jim's thoughts on art and especially his own painting style. He always paints quickly and with a lot of energy. Having worked for many years in an artistic, technical industry, it was the everyday attention to detail that made Jim seek an outlet to express his talent more freely. In 1997 Jim studied art for several months under Clarence Betleyoun who is an accomplished painter and instructor. He concluded his study and continued to developed his palette knife technique on his own.

Jim, after a short time, began displaying his paintings locally, but it was exhibiting at his friend's mother's gallery The Stofko-Dixon Line that transformed Jim from being a "weekend hobbyist" to a true painter. One evening, Jim received a call from Terri and Wayne Wetendorf who were opening a new restaurant in Forsyth, Georgia called Grits Cafe. They had stopped at the Stofko-Dixon Line, seen his work and wanted it in their restaurant. So with a hand shake they took everything he had available, both in the gallery, and his home.

Jim continued to paint and exhibit in galleries and exhibitions both locally and regionally over the next 15 years until a 2012 fire at Grits Cafe destroyed both the restaurant and years of Jim's work. He did not paint for months and even considered not painting in the future. Later that year the Wetendorfs asked Jim to hang new paintings in the rebuilt Grits Cafe. Jim hit his "reset button" and began painting again, this time with more enthusiasm than before.

Jim has been represented by the Dan Goad Gallery on St. Simons Island, Georgia, Hollis Gallery in Chattanooga, Tennessee, and The Stofko-Dixon Line in Bolingbroke, Georgia. He has exhibited at The Stofko-Dixon Line, The Gallery at Theatre Macon, The Macon Arts Alliance Gallery, the Georgia National Fair, and the Quinlan Visual Arts Center.

His work is in corporate and private collections in the United States, Canada, and the U.K.

It was this renewed enthusiasm for painting and his love of Led Zeppelin that prompted Jim to reach out to Scott and Ruth Roe at Bron Yr Aur. What began as a simple request for the use of photographs quickly developed into "The Bron Yr Aur Project". Scott described the whole thing as "organically coming together" and for the first time since Jimmy Page and Robert Plant's famed visit to the Cottage some 40 years ago, an effort is being made to honor the quiet little cottage that is hidden in the hills surrounding Machynlleth. Jim's works are the first commissioned paintings of Bron Yr Aur. Jim renders his subjects with a vivid impasto effect. Using a limited palette of colors, he works in both oil and acrylic applying the paint with knives, brushes and even paper towels, preferring to use pure color from the tube with little mixing on the palette.

Jim Stallings

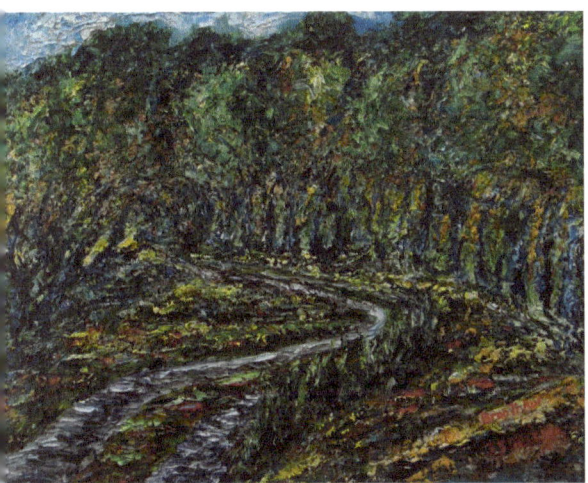

'The Road To Bron Yr Aur'
16"x20" (Cat no: JS001)
Oil on canvas - £900

Available as 16" x 20" printed
reproduction
£100 (Cat No: JS001/P)

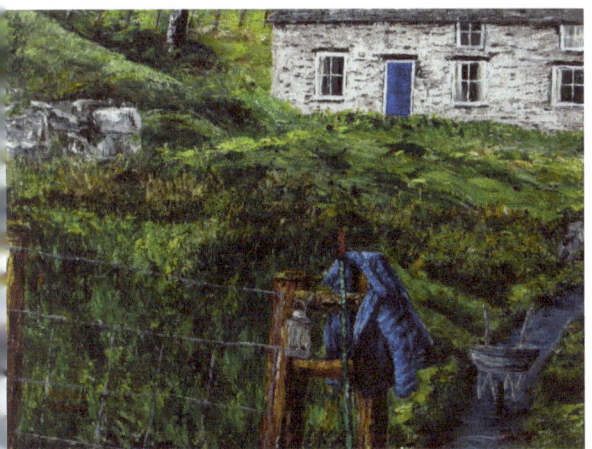

'Ruth's Coat'
30"x40" (Cat no: JS002)
Acrylic on canvas - £1400

Available as 16" x 20" high
quality printed reproduction
£100 (Cat No: JS002/P)

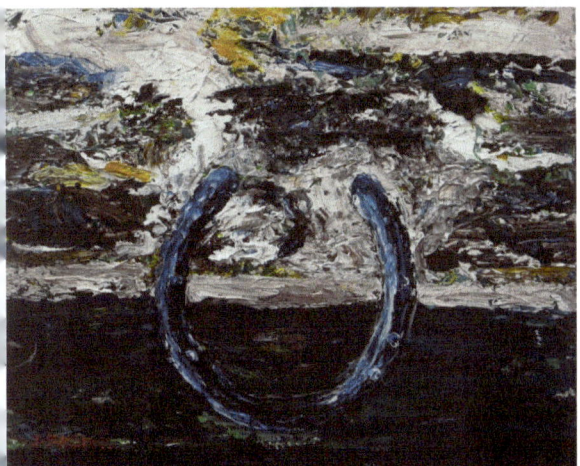

'Luck'
16"x20" (Cat no: JS003)
Acrylic on canvas - £900

Available as 16" x 20" high
quality printed reproduction
£100 (Cat No: JS003/P)

Jim Stallings

'Hillside'
30"x40" (Cat no: JS004)
Acrylic on canvas -
£1400

Available as 16" x
20" printed
reproduction
£100 (Cat No: JS004/P)

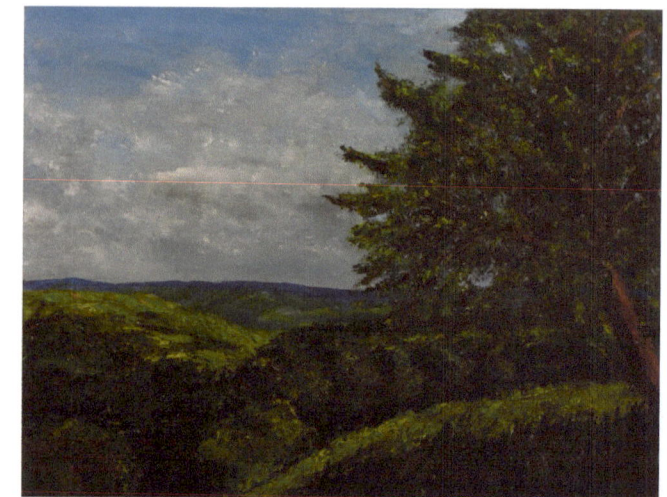

'direction'
16"x20" (Cat no: JS005)
Oil on canvas NFS

Available as 16" x
20" printed
reproduction
£100 (Cat No: JS005/P)

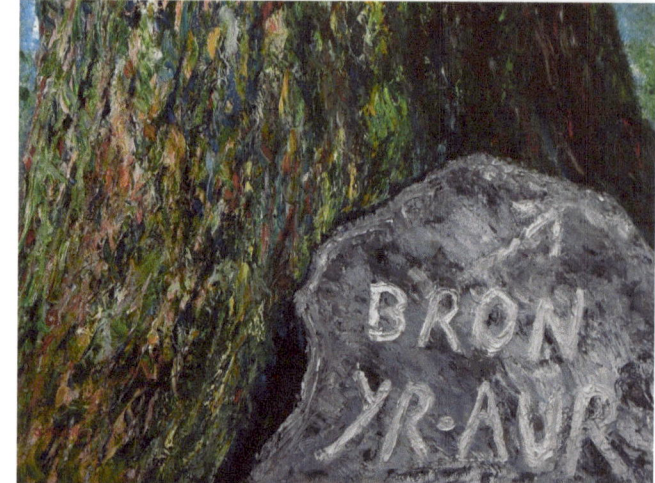

'Boncyff'
30"x40" (Cat no: JS006)
Acrylic on canvas
£1400

Available as 16" x 20"
high quality printed
reproduction
£100 (Cat No: JS006/P)

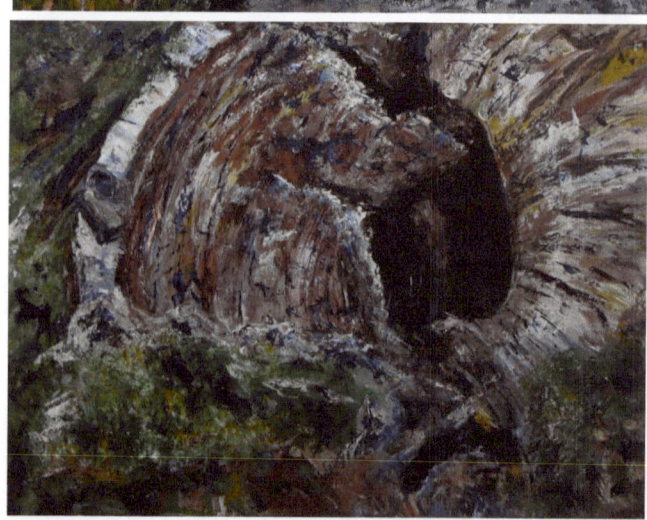

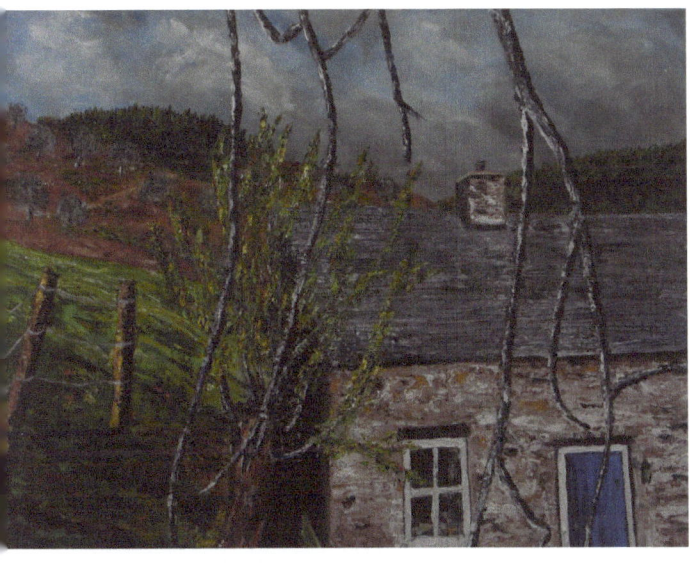

Jim Stallings

'Cloudy Morning'
30"x40" (Cat no: JS007)
Acrylic on canvas
£1400

Available as 16" x 20"
printed reproduction
£100 (Cat No: JS007/P)

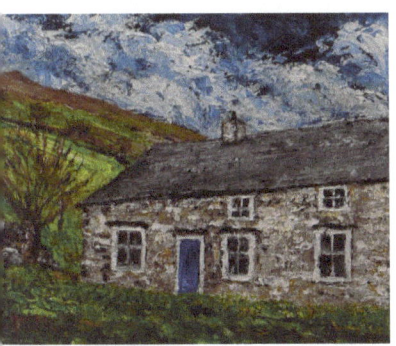

'Jersey View'
16"x20" (Cat no: JS008)
Acrylic on canvas - £900

Available as 16" x 20" printed
reproduction
£100 (Cat No: JS008/P)

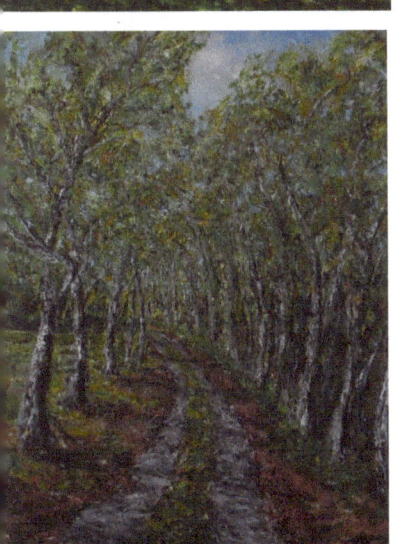

'Tree Canopy at Bron Yr Aur'
40"x30" (Cat no: JS009)
Acrylic on canvas - £1400

Available as 16" x 20" high
quality printed reproduction
£100 (Cat No: JS009/P)

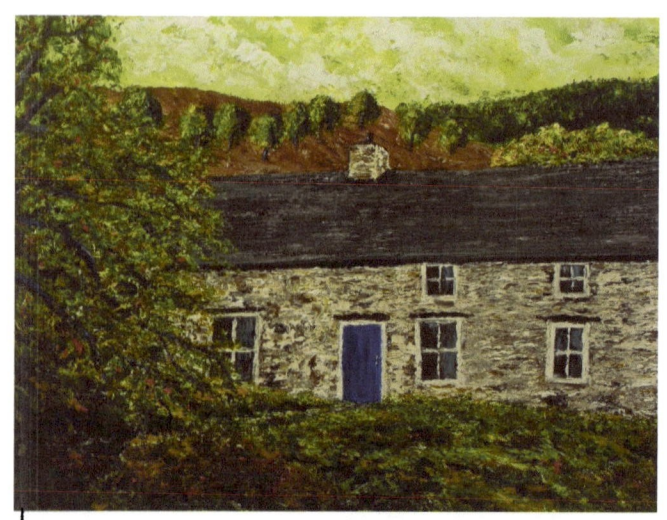

Jim Stallings

'Bron Yr Aur'
30"x40"
(Cat no: JS014)
Oil on canvas -
£1400

Available as 16" x 20" printed reproduction
£100 (Cat No: JS014/P)

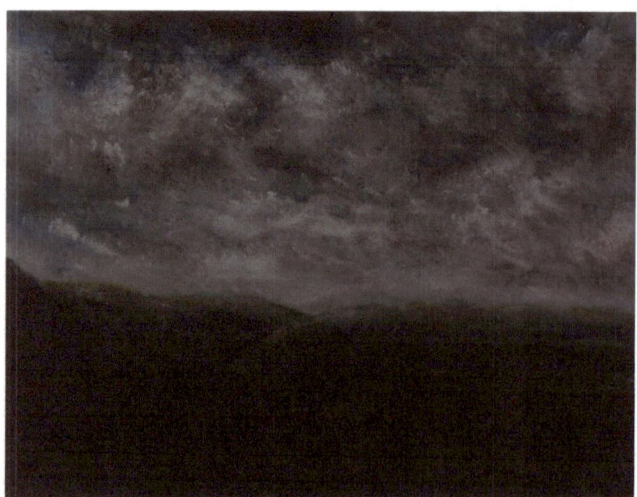

'The Misty
Mountains'
30"x40" (Cat no:
JS012)
Acrylic on canvas -
£1400

Available as 16" x 20" printed reproduction
£100 (Cat No: JS012/P)

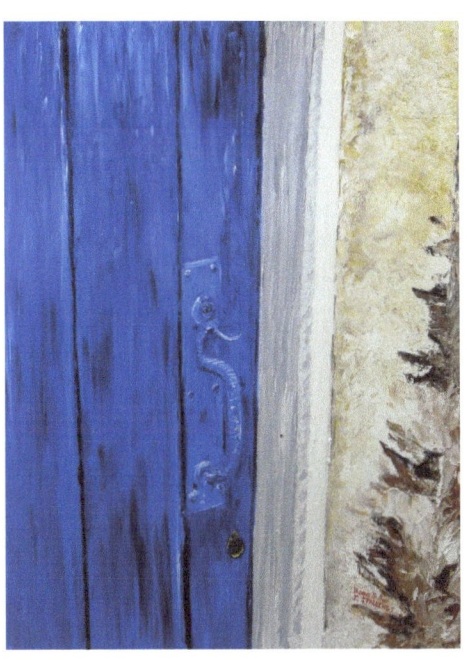

Jim Stallings

'Ffrindiau' - 40"x30"?
(Cat no: JS013)
Oil? on canvas - £1400?

Available as 16" x 20" high quality printed reproduction £100 (Cat No: JS013/P)

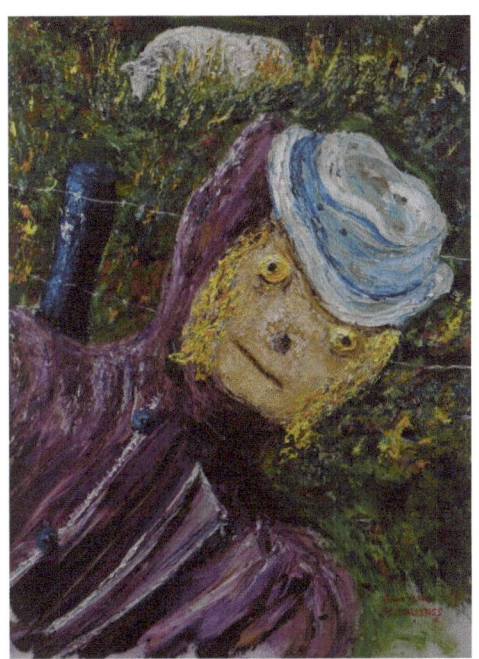

'Blimey Guvna' - 40"x30"
(Cat no: JS010)
Oil on canvas - £1400

Available as 16" x 20" high quality printed reproduction £100 (Cat No: JS010/P)

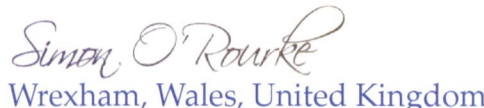

Simon O'Rourke
Wrexham, Wales, United Kingdom

Simon O'Rourke is a Liverpool born Illustration graduate, who stumbled across wood carving through working as a tree surgeon. Simon quickly realised the potential of the chainsaw in producing large scale, high impact sculpture in a short space of time. The speed and energy of this art is echoed in the surface texture, and can be used to enhance the movement of a sculpture.

Simon's passion for classical sculpture has pushed his boundaries in this artform, and he loves the fact that something beautiful can be produced using this potentially violent and destructive machine. His work is a mixture of life studies and works of fantasy. He aims to give each piece he creates a narrative, and wants the viewer to walk away feeling they've just caught a glimpse of an active scene.

Simon produces commissions for private and corporate customers, and has also worked with school groups and local authorities to encourage new and emerging artists. He gives talks and demonstrations and is involved in a Welsh Assembly Government initiative promoting entrepreneurship and running businesses within schools and FE colleges.

He has also competed in competitions around the world, winning several awards at an international level.

www.treecarving.co.uk

01978 312477

07886 881815

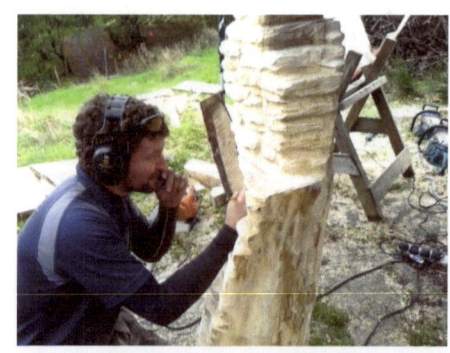

Simon O'Rourke

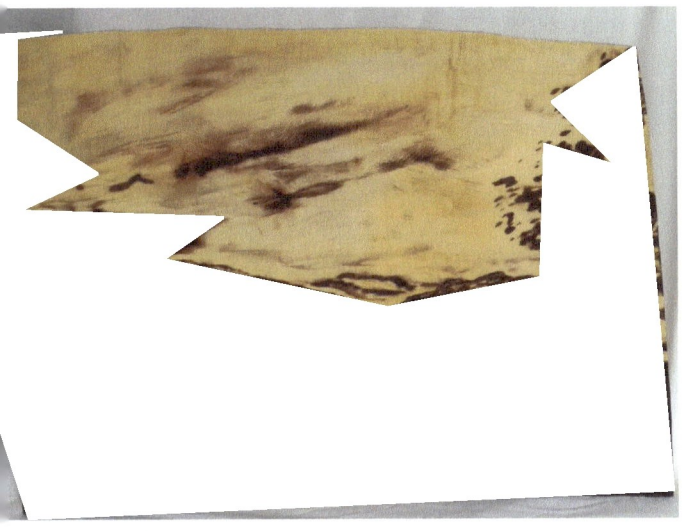

'darkening sky'
(Cat no: SOR001)

Carved 'Bron Yr Aur Sycamore' W663mm x H469mm xD36mm / £480 Available as 16" x 20" printed reproduction (Cat No: SOR001/P) / £100

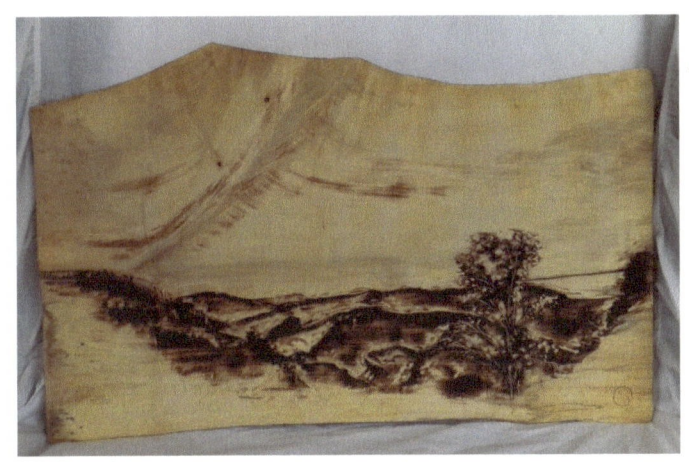

'autumn light'
(Cat no: SOR002)

Carved 'Bron Yr Aur Sycamore' W760mm x H467mm x D35mm/ £480 Available as 16" x 20" printed reproduction (Cat no: SOR002/P) / £100

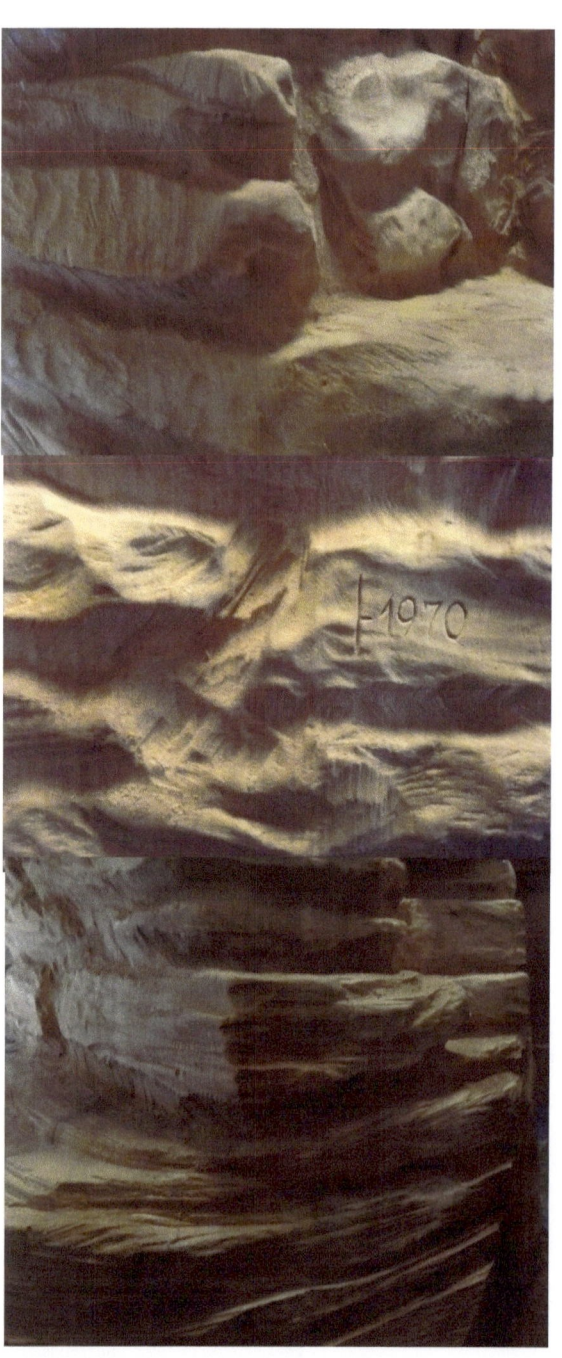

Simon O'Rourke

'The stones remember'
Cat no: SOR003

'Bron Yr Aur Sycamore'
sculpture
W550mm x H1290mm x D330mm
£1800

Photographs show details from sections of the larger work. Please get in touch if you wish to view the piece or see further images and video footage.

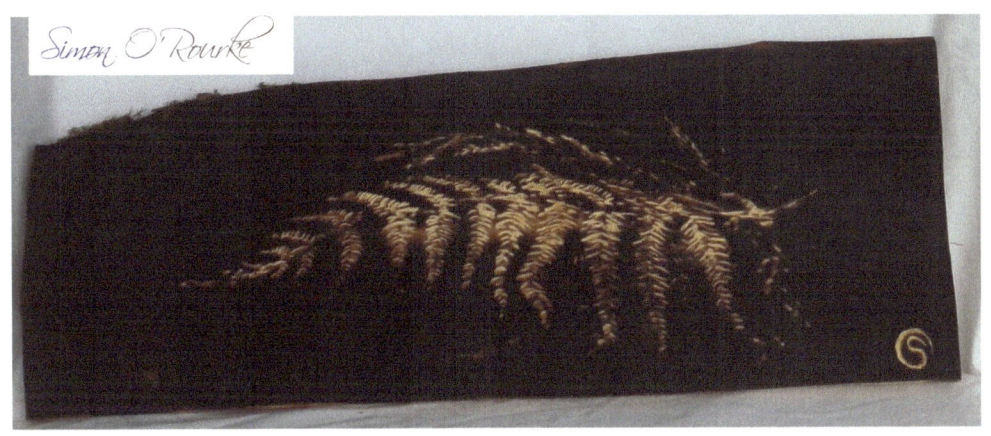

Simon O'Rourke

Bron Yr Aur Fern 02 (Cat no: SOR004)
Carved 'Bron Yr Aur Sycamore' (W659mm x H238mm x D32mm) / £360
Available as 16" x 20" printed reproduction (Cat No: SOR004/P)/ £100

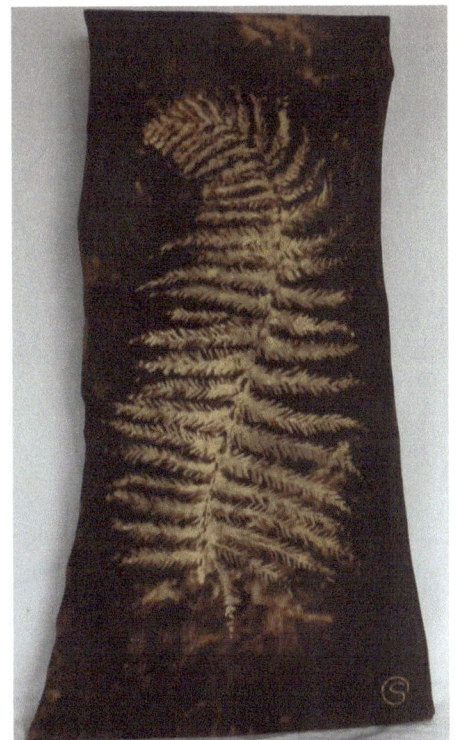

Bron Yr Aur Fern 01
(Cat no: SOR005)
Carved 'Bron Yr Aur Sycamore'
W390mm x H650mm x D32mm /
£480

Available 16" x 20"
printed reproduction
(Cat No: SOR005/P) / £100

Simon O'Rourke

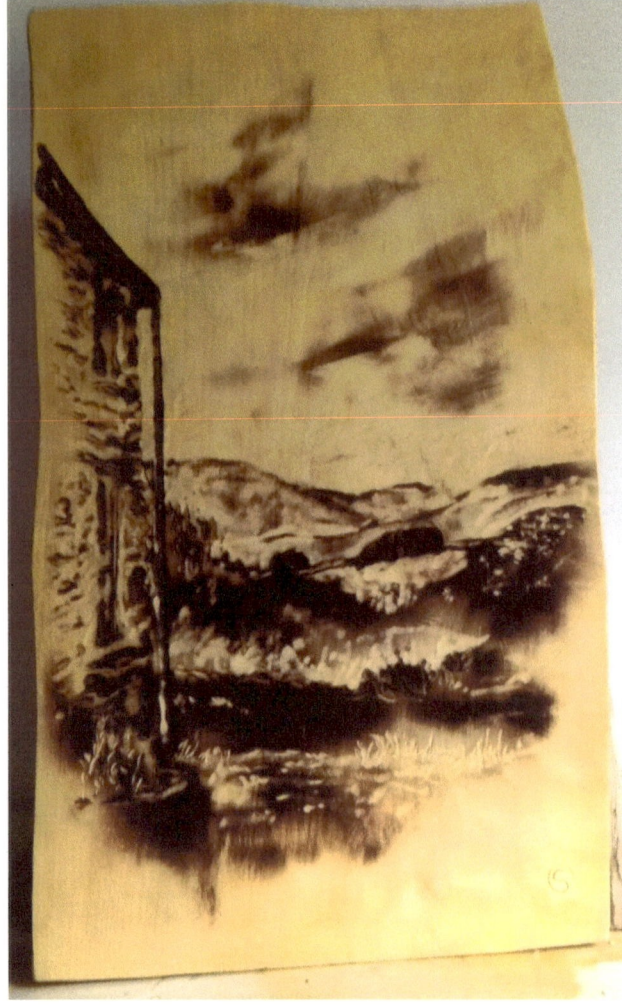

'a glimmer of sun'
(Cat no SOR006)

Carved 'Bron Yr Aur Sycamore'
W550mm x H1'290 x D350mm / £480

Available 16" x 20" printed reproduction (Cat No: SOR006/P) / £100

Nathan Woods
Wrexham, Wales, United Kingdom

Nathan Woods...
...is a happy artist. He got to soak up the inspirational
surroundings of Bron yr aur and produce this set of work there. He
also played some bad guitar. Nathan trained in illustration, but has
worked with tattoo-machines, computers and chainsaws in his art
since. Separately. A bit like the A-team with less explosions and
more draughtsmanship

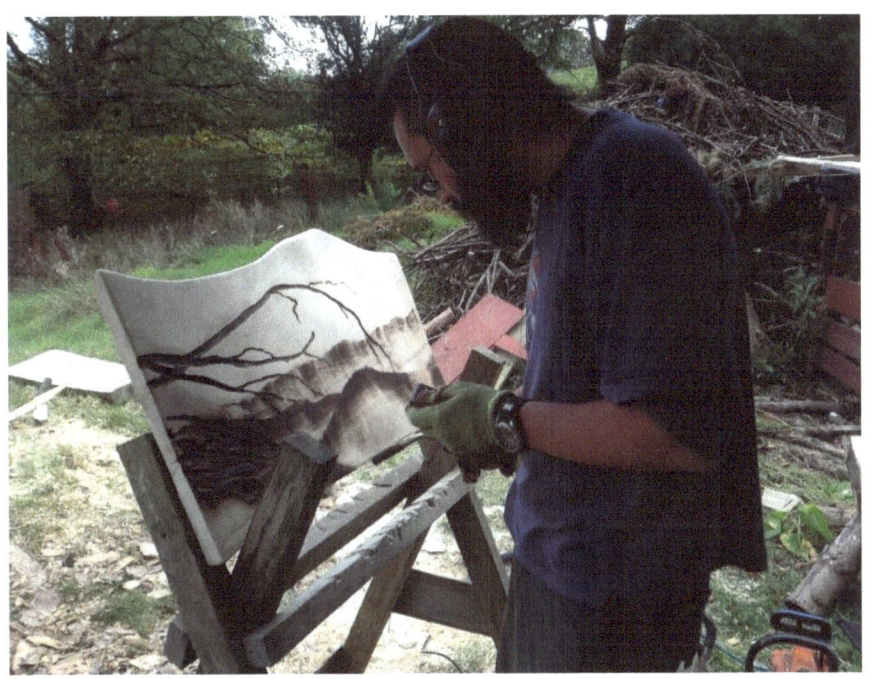

Nathan Woods

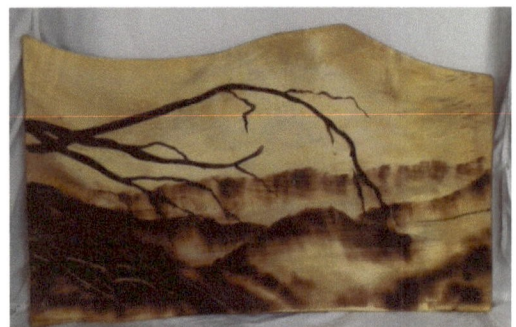

'The front aspect'
(Cat no: NW001)

Carved 'Bron Yr Aur
Sycamore'
W310mm x H784mm x D32mm
£300

Available as 16" x 20"
printed reproduction
£100 (Cat No: NW001/P)

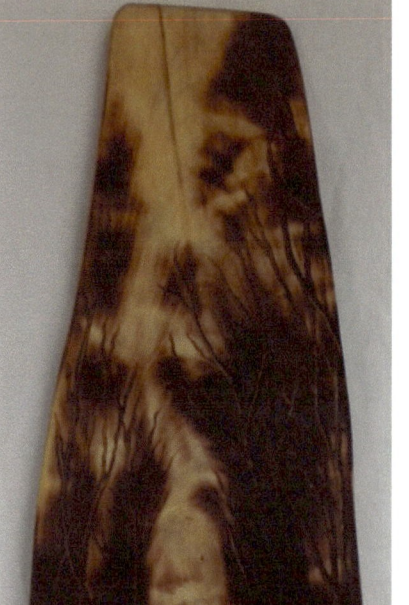

'Bron yr aur approach'
(Cat no: NW002)

Carved 'Bron Yr Aur
Sycamore'
W310mm x H784mm x D32mm
£300

Available as 16" x 20"
printed reproduction
£100 (Cat No: NW002/P)

Nathan Woods

'Hazel viewpoint'
(Cat no: NW003)

Carved Bron Yr Aur Sycamore
W765mm x H383mm x D43mm
£360

Available as 16" x 20"
printed reproduction
£100 (Cat No: NW003/P)

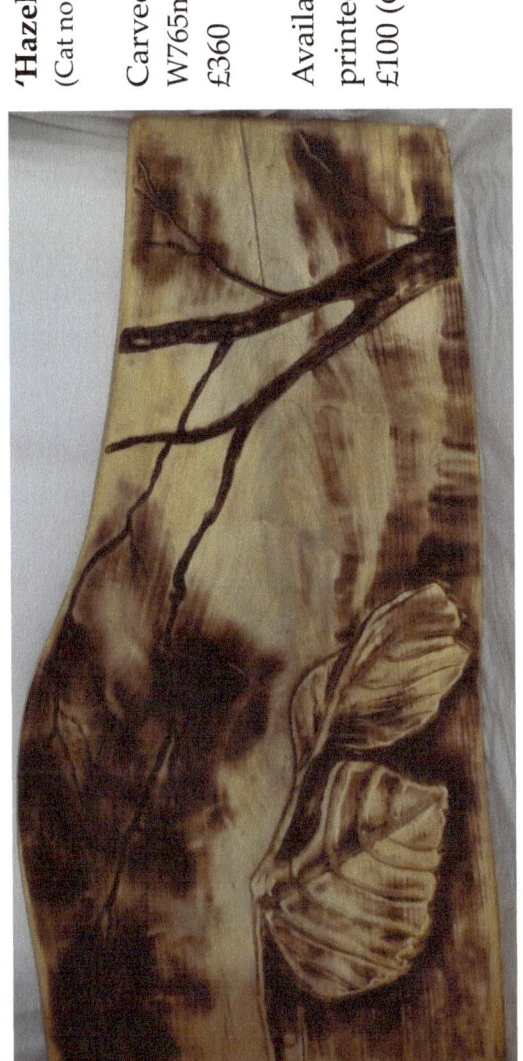

Ruth Roe
Machynlleth, Wales

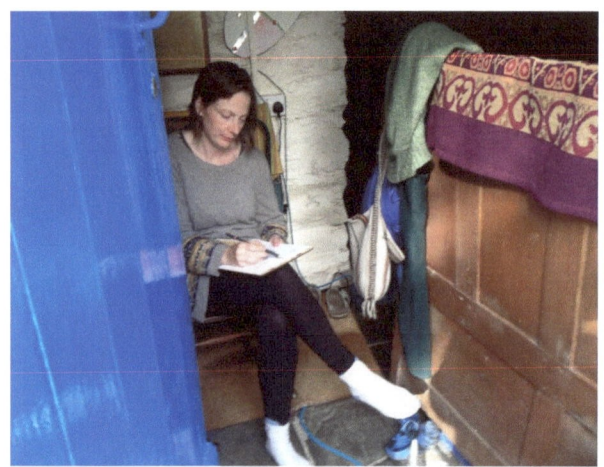

Influenced for a lifetime by the sights and atmosphere of Bron yr aur, Ruth studied Art at the University of Warwick, with her degree show drawing inspiration from nearby ruins of a similar dwelling, which hide away in the forest. Ruth's contributions to the Bron yr aur project represent a truly unique assemblage, combining current vistas with her own memories and, most notably, recollections made by her Mother, from 1970.

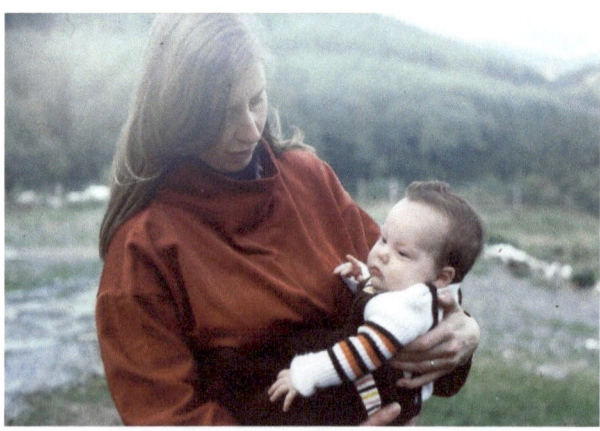

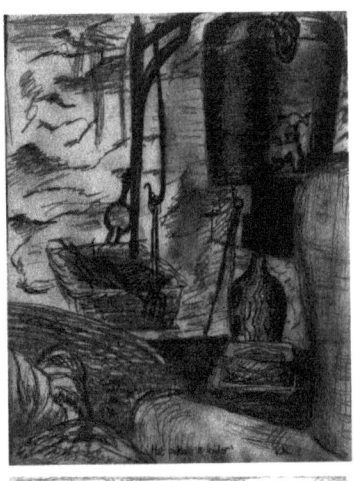

'Hot pokers & Cider'
(Cat no: RR001)
Charcoal - £40

Available as 12″ x 8″ mounted print
£25 (Cat No: RR001/P)

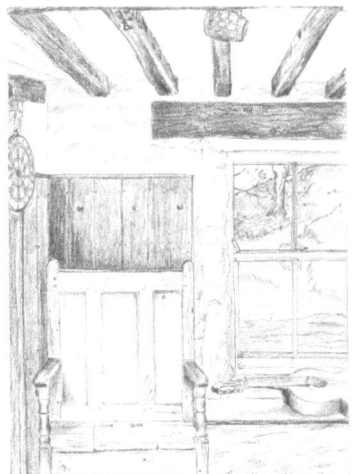

'Then and now'
(Cat no: RR002)
Charcoal - £75

Available as 12″ x 8″ mounted print
£25 (Cat No: RR002/P)

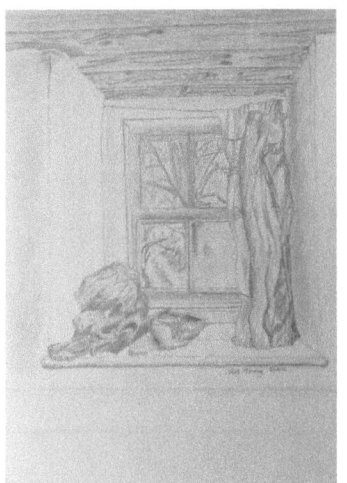

'Next morning'
(Cat no: RR003)
Charcoal - £40

Available as 12″ x 9″ mounted print
£25 (Cat No: RR003/P)

White Dove
Machynlleth, Wales, United Kingdom

White Dove has worked prolifically for seven years, most recently developing an excellent sense of scale and place. Her first commercial work sold locally in 2011, in the form of greetings cards. Last year her crayon-work was successful in reaching the second round of the Welsh Urdd Eisteddfod, and her painting won first place in the Pennal village show.

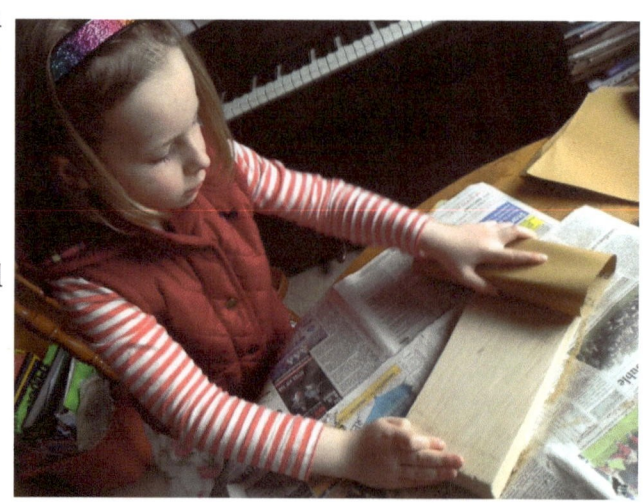

The Bron yr aur Project is thrilled to have produced this collaborative piece with White Dove and Simon O'Rourke, in which is captured both the wilderness and cosiness of this historic cottage, by its youngest resident.

White Dove

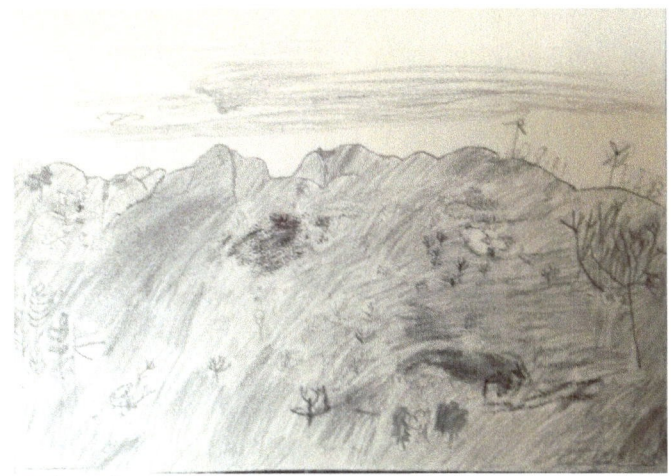

'The view' (Cat no: CR/002)
Pencil sketch £75
Available as 12" x 8" printed reproduction
£30 (Cat No: CR002/P)

White Dove & Simon O'Rourke

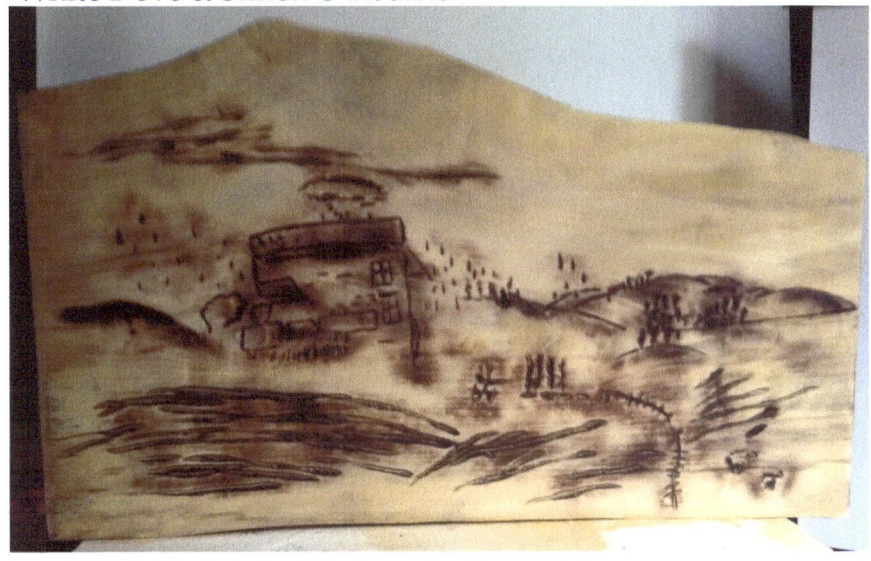

'Home' (Cat no: SOR/CR001) Carved Sycamore - £595
Available as 16" x 20" printed reproduction
£100 (Cat No: SO/CR/001/P)

Ben Kennedy
Birmingham, England

Drawing and painting since childhood, Birmingham based artist Ben Kennedy is for the most part self-taught. His enthusiastic and eclectic embrace of artistic expression across the years is self-evident. Ben's more recent work is a revealing 'tell' on inspirations drawn from 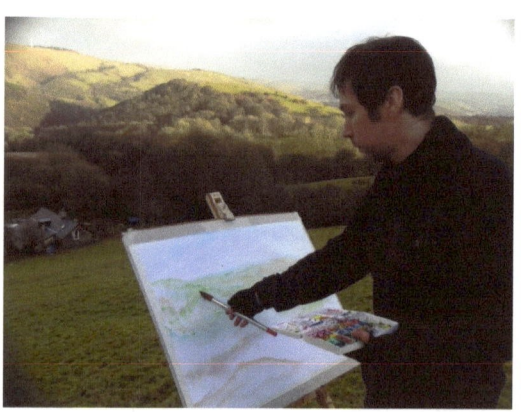 dynamic environments, and from the extensive photographic, Art and graphic collections at the Library of Birmingham where he works.

Formerly guitarist with UK band Liner, Ben's musical inspirations now segue neatly into his recent studies of the history and beauty of hill-top cottage Bron yr Aur, near Machynlleth, and the surrounding area. Currently working on a series of large-scale charcoal landscapes, his goal is to render a tableau of emotionally powerful impressionist scenes.

He draws much influence from Turner's late works and pre Raphaelite art.

www.facebook.com/BenKennedyArt

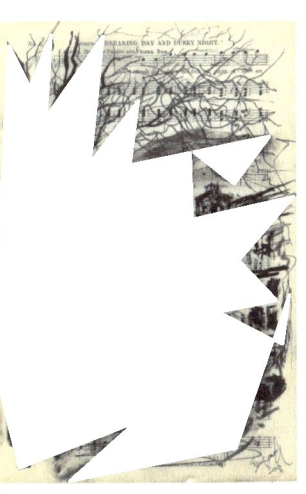

'Breaking day and dusky night'
(Cat no: BK012)
Ink on music manuscript - £120
9.5"x 6.5" / mounted 12"x8"

Available as 12" x 8" mounted print
£30 (Cat No: BK012/P)

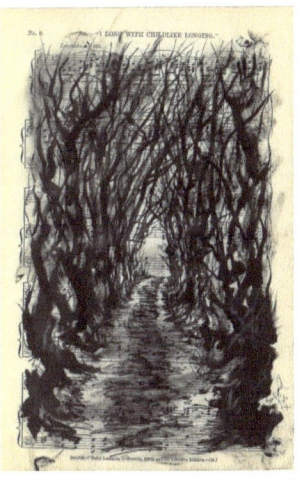

'I long with childlike longing'
(Cat no: BK013)
Ink on music manuscript - £75
9.5"x 6.5" / mounted 12"x8"
Available as 12" x 8" mounted print
£30(Cat No: BK013/P)

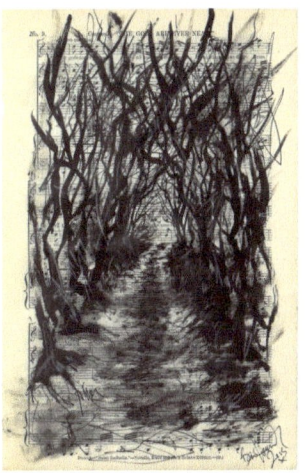

'The gods are ever near'
(Cat no: BK014)
Ink on music manuscript - £75
9.5"x 6.5" / mounted 12"x8"
Available as 12" x 8" mounted print
£30 (Cat No: BK014/P)

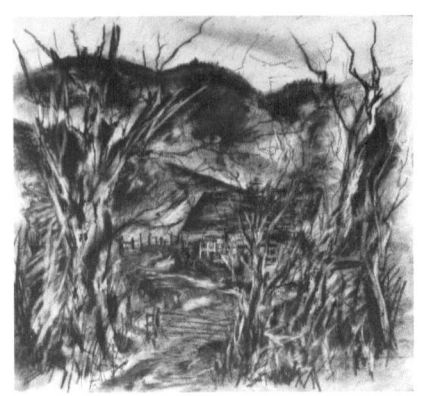

'Bron Yr Aur in WInter'
(Cat no: BK001
Charcoal and ink - £150
23"x20" /Mounted 27"x 23"

Available as 12" x 8" mounted print
£30 (Cat No: BK0001/P

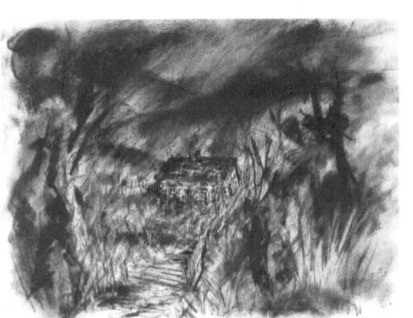

'Storm'
(Cat no: BK002
Charcoal and ink - £75
12"x17" / Mounted: 16"x20"

Available as 12" x 8" mounted print
£30(Cat No: BK002/P

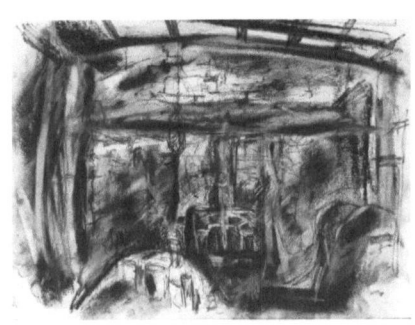

'Where we sat'
(Cat no: BK003
Charcoal and Ink - £75
12"x17" / Mounted: 16"x20"

Available as 12" x 8" mounted print
£30 (Cat No: BK003/P)

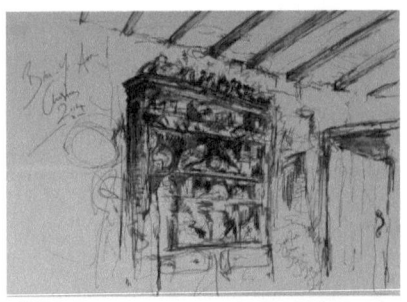

'Dresser'
(Cat no: BK004
Chacoal and ink- £75
12"x17" / Mounted: 16"x20"
Available as 12" x 9" mounted print
£30 (Cat No: BK004/P)

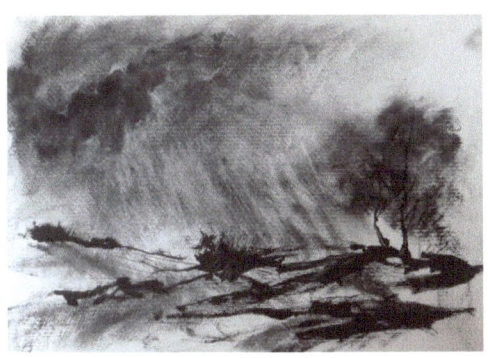

'Evening rain'
(Cat no: BK015)
Charcoal and ink - £75
14"x10" / mounted 16"x12"
Available as 12" x 8" mounted print
£30 (Cat No: BK015/P)

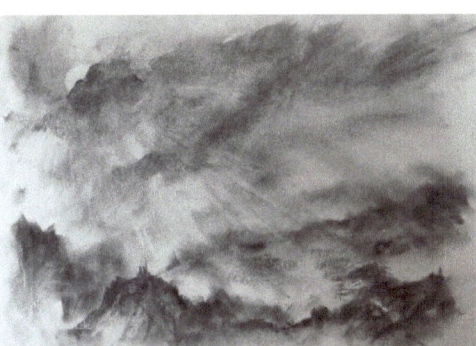

'Morning mist'
(Cat no: BK016)
Charcoal - £75
16"x11"/ mounted 18"x14"
Available as 12" x 8" mounted print
£30(Cat No: BK016/P)

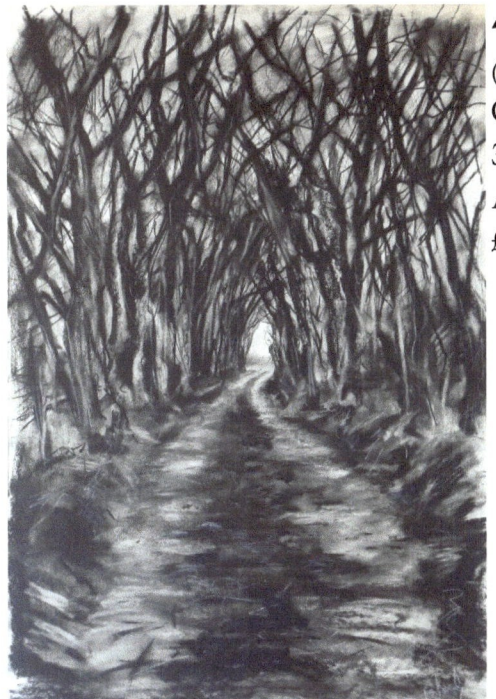

'The path to Bron Yr Aur 1'
(Cat no: BK008)
Charcoal and ink - £220
32"x22" / mounted 34"x24"
Available as 12" x 8" mounted print
£30 (Cat No: BK008/P)

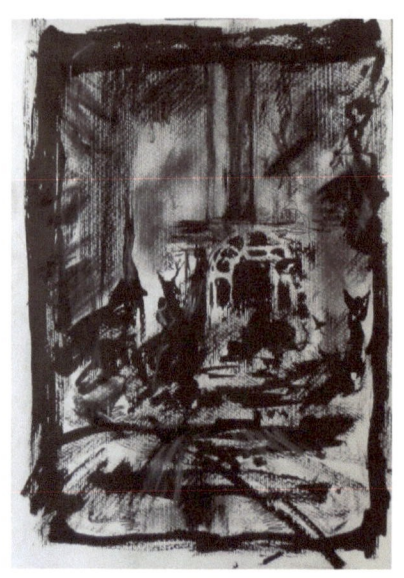

'Black cats'
(Cat no: BK011)
Charcoal and ink - £75
14" x 10"/ Mounted 16"x12"
Available as 12" x 8" mounted print
£30 (Cat No: BK011/P)

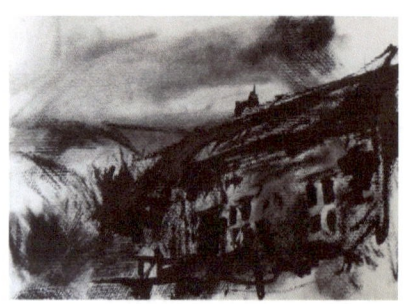

'Bron Yr Aur in ink'
(Cat no: BK010)
Charcoal and ink - £75
14" x 10"/ mounted 16"x12"
Available as 12" x 8" mounted print
£30(Cat No: BK010/P)

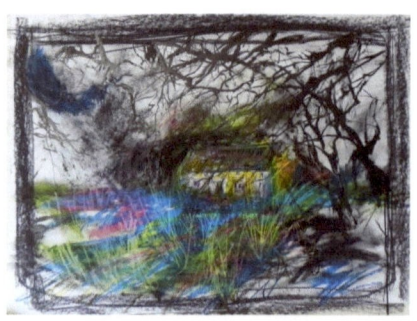

'Bron Yr Aur by dusk'
(Cat no: BK009)
Ink, charcoal and oil pastels - £220
32"x22" / Mounted 32"x24"
Available as 12" x 8" mounted print
£30 (Cat No: BK009/P)

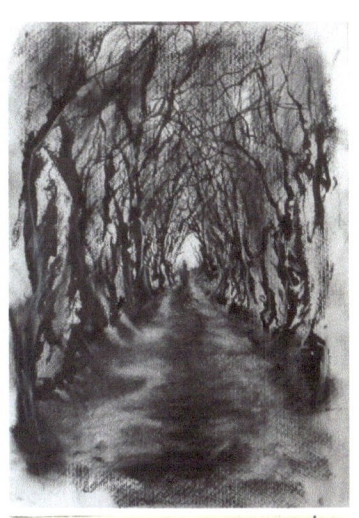

'The path to Bron Yr Aur 2'
(Cat no: BK006
Charcoal and ink - £75
14" x 10" / mounted 16"x12"
Available as 12" x 8" mounted print
£30 (Cat No: BK006/P)

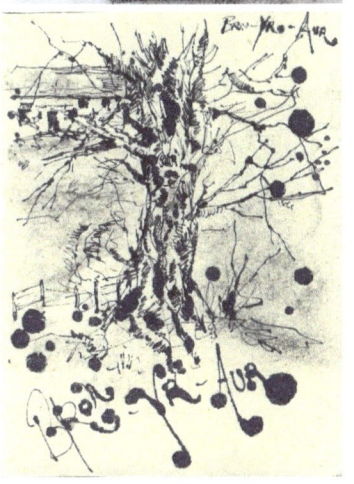

'Sycamore'
(Cat no: BK005)
Ink - £80
6.5x4" / Mounted 8x6"
Available as 12" x 8" mounted print
£30(Cat No: BK005/P)

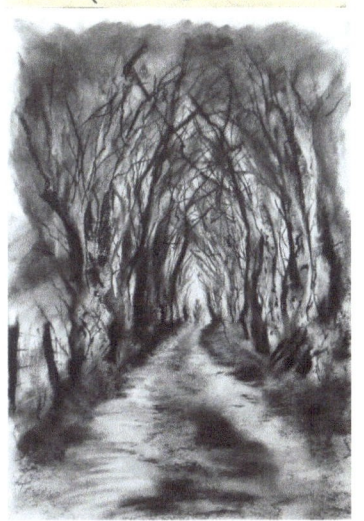

'The path to Bron Yr Aur 3'
(Cat no: BK007)
Charcoal and ink - £75
16"x11" / Mounted 18"x14"
Available as 12" x 8" mounted print
£30 (Cat No: BK007/P)

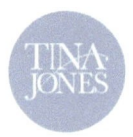

Tina Jones
Machynlleth, Wales, United Kingdom

Tina Jones is a professional photographer based in Machynlleth.

'It's the cottage below where Led Zeppelin came to stay in the very early 70's, penning some beautiful tunes. One of the reasons I came to visit this place, and though it's not the reason
I stayed, looking at this photograph always takes me back to that fateful visit! '

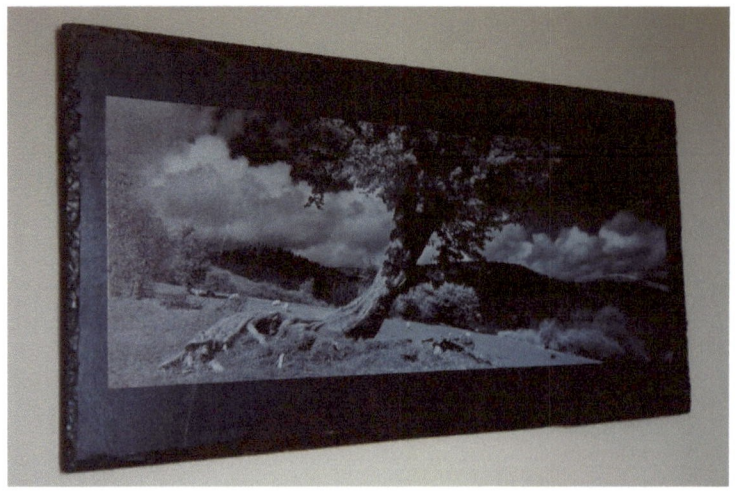

'Hawthorn above Bron Yr Aur'
(Cat no: TJ001)
High quality print on Welsh slate - 24"x12" - £220

High quality framed print - 21"x12" - £185

www.tinajones.co.uk

Scott Roe

Machynlleth, Wales, United Kingdom

Scott's 'raggedy-hotch-potch' artistic career has included circus, theatre, music and more static forms of visual art.
Living at Bron Yr Aur has brought the emergence of a more visually creative process, experimenting with natural pigments made from

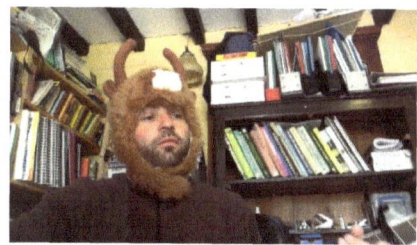 lichen and plants, and resulting in photographic prints and images printed onto wood sourced in location, evoking the gentle, magical atmosphere so connected with this historic place.

info@thegreenphoenix.co.uk
www.bronyraur.com
www.facebook.com/therealbronyraur
www.saatchiart.com/bronyraur

Scott Roe

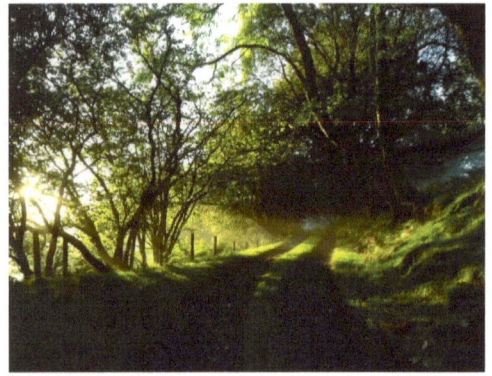

'Bron Yr Aur Golden Light'
(Cat no: SR006)
Limited Edition mounted
photographic print
 8" x 6" / £28
12" x 9" / £30
Limited to 100 prints

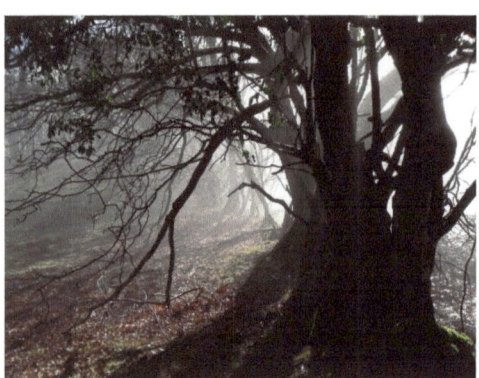

'Bron Yr Aur Shroud'
(Cat no: SR009)
Limited Edition mounted
photographic print
 8" x 6" / £28
12" x 9" / £30
Limited to 100 prints

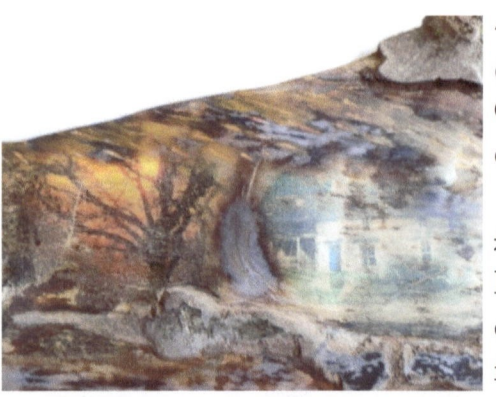

'Transformation'
(Cat no: SR010)
Oil, acrylics and ink prints on
carved Bron Yr Aur Sycamore

£625
Illustration does not show
complete piece, shows detail
from work only.

Scott Roe

'Bron Yr Aur Misty Mountain'
(Cat no: SR001)
Limited Edition mounted
photographic print
8" x 6" / £28
12" x 9" / £30
Limited to 100 prints

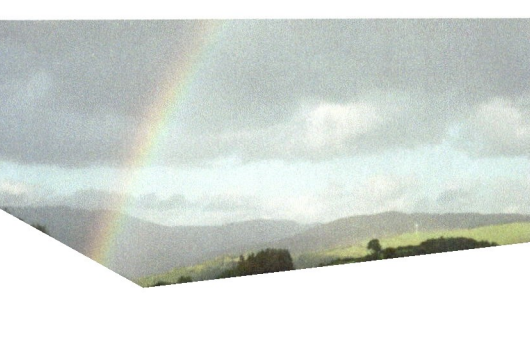

'Bron Yr Aur Rainbow'
(Cat no: SR002)
Limited Edition mounted
photographic print
8" x 6" / £28
12" x 9" / £30
Limited to 100 prints

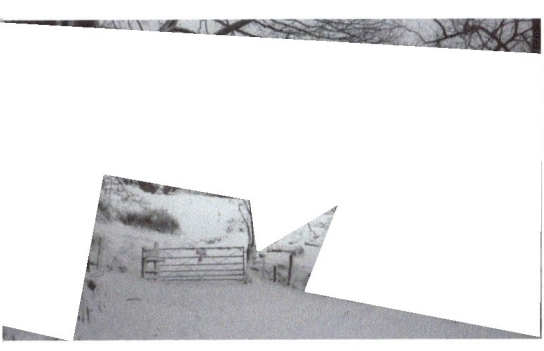

'Bron Yr Aur Winter Wonderland'
(Cat no: SR003)
Limited Edition mounted
photographic print
8" x 6" / £28
12" x 9" / £30
Limited to 100 prints

Scott Roe

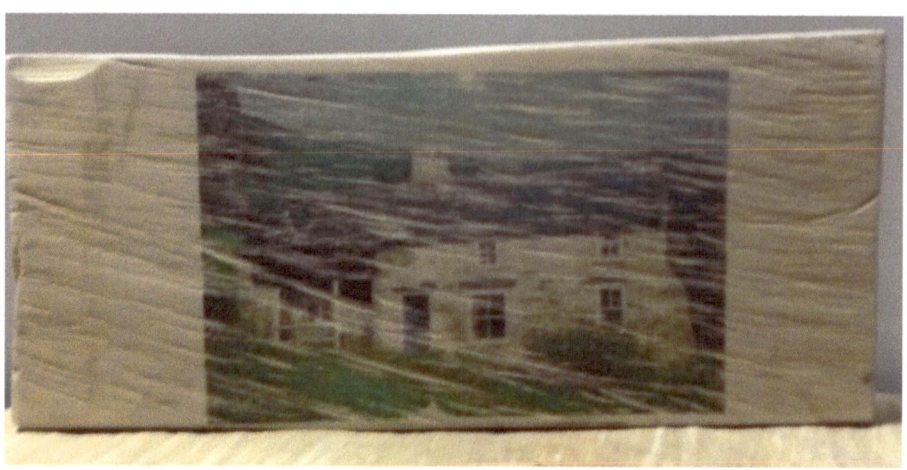

'1971'
(Cat no: SR004)
One-off print on 'Bron Yr Aur Sycamore
W292 x H189 x D310 £75

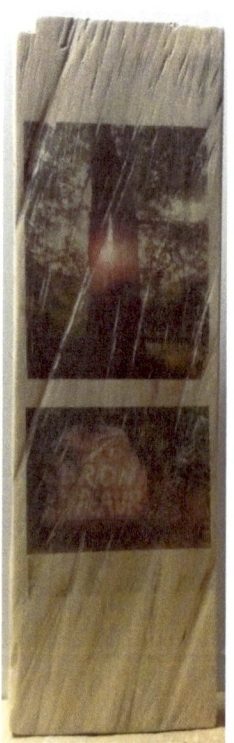

'Morning light'
(Cat no: SR005)
One-off print on Bron Yr Aur Sycamore
W11 x H370 x D40
£75

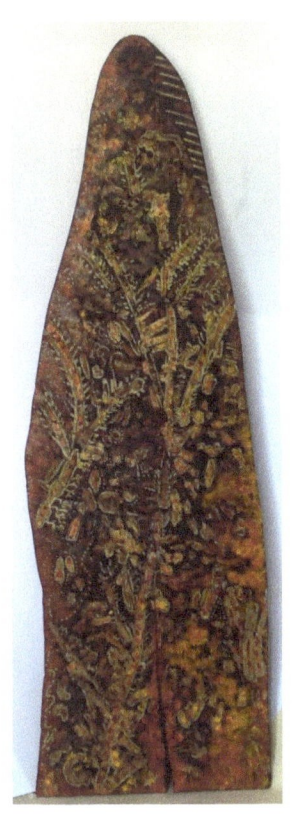

'Icebracken'
(Cat no: SR007)
Oil, Acrylic and ink on carved
'Bron Yr Aur' Sycamore

£290

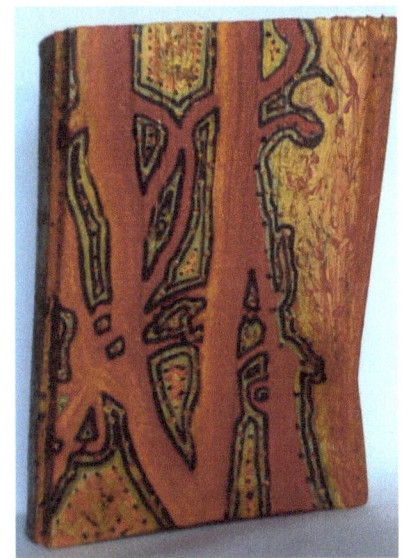

'Firetree'
(Cat no: SR008)

Acrylic, Oil and ink on 'Bron Yr
Aur' Sycamore.

£160

Exhibitions and outlets

Moma Wales
Launch Event - 12:00 Midday
25th April 2015
Featuring the work of Jim Stallings

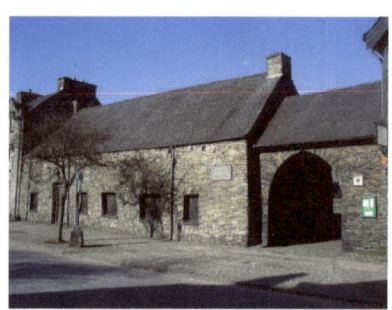

The Tabernacle
Heol Penrallt
Machynlleth
Powys SY20 8AJ

Tel (+44) 01654 703355
Fax (+44) 01654 702160

The Owain Glyndwr Centre
Launch Event - 10:00
25th April 2015

Featuring the work of Jim Stallings, Simon O'Rourke, Nathan Woods,
Ben Kennedy, Tina Jones, Ruth Roe, Scott Roe and White Dove

Canolfan Owain Glyndwr Cyf.
Heol Maengwyn,
Machynlleth,
Powys
SY20 8EE
01654 702932

Online sales and information
www.bronyraur.com
www.saatchiart.com/bronyraur
www.facebook.com/therealbronyraur
sales@bronyraur.com

Related websites, pages and information sources

Jim Stallings
www.jstallings.com

Simon O'Rourke
www.treecarving.co.uk
www.facebook.com/simonorourketreecarving

Ben Kennedy
www.facebook.com/BenKennedyArt

Tina Jones
www.tinajones.co.uk

Scott Roe
www.saatchiart.com/bronyraur

The Owain Glyndwr Centre (Ancient Parliament building)
www.canolfanglyndwr.org

Moma Wales
www.momawales.org.uk
www.facebook.com/MOMAWales
twitter.com/momawales

Official Bron Yr Aur pages
www.bronyraur.com
www.facebook.com/therealbronyraur

www.ingramcontent.com/pod-product-compliance
Lightning Source LLC
Chambersburg PA
CBHW040819200526
45159CB00024B/3046